Stained Glass
COLOR BY NUMBERS

Stained Glass
COLOR BY NUMBERS

David
Woodroffe

SIRIUS

SIRIUS

This edition published in 2021 by Sirius Publishing, a division of
Arcturus Publishing Limited,
26/27 Bickels Yard, 151–153 Bermondsey Street,
London SE1 3HA

ISBN: 978-1-3988-0932-1
CH008592NT
Supplier 29, Date 0521, Print run 11408

Printed in China

Introduction

For hundreds of years stained-glass images have adorned buildings and objects of all kinds, from great cathedrals to Tiffany lamps, and the process of coloring glass is one that stretches back to the times of the Ancient Egyptians and Romans. Nowadays, however, new artists are letting their imagination take flight and producing wonderful new designs and three-dimensional objects using this ancient skill.

This delightful collection of color-by-number images draws on beautiful examples of stained glass, including traditional compositions and heraldic shields as well as pretty images of wildlife and flowers, geometric patterns, and modern abstract designs. As you might expect, there is a kaleidoscope of color to relish within these pages.

If you are new to coloring by numbers, it is worth labeling your colored pencils or pens with the relevant numbers that you will find in the key on the inside flap at the back of this book. However, there is no obligation to follow the key if you don't want to; you can let your imagination run riot and produce a color scheme all of your own to complete these charming images.

Enjoy!

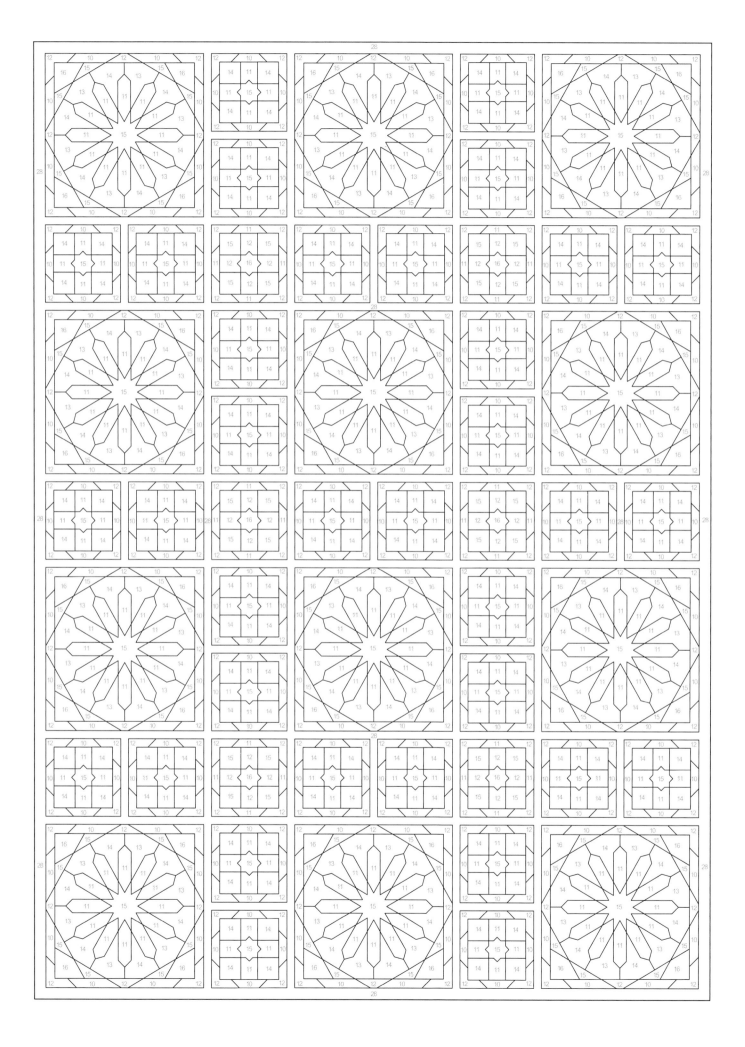

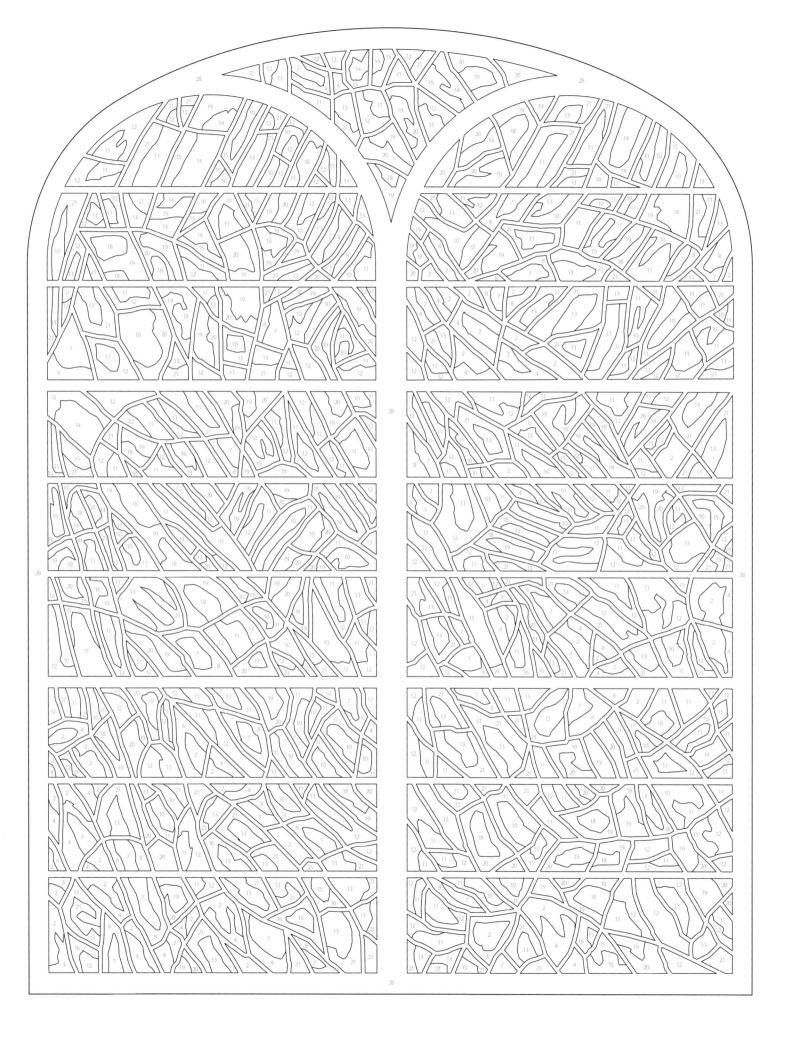

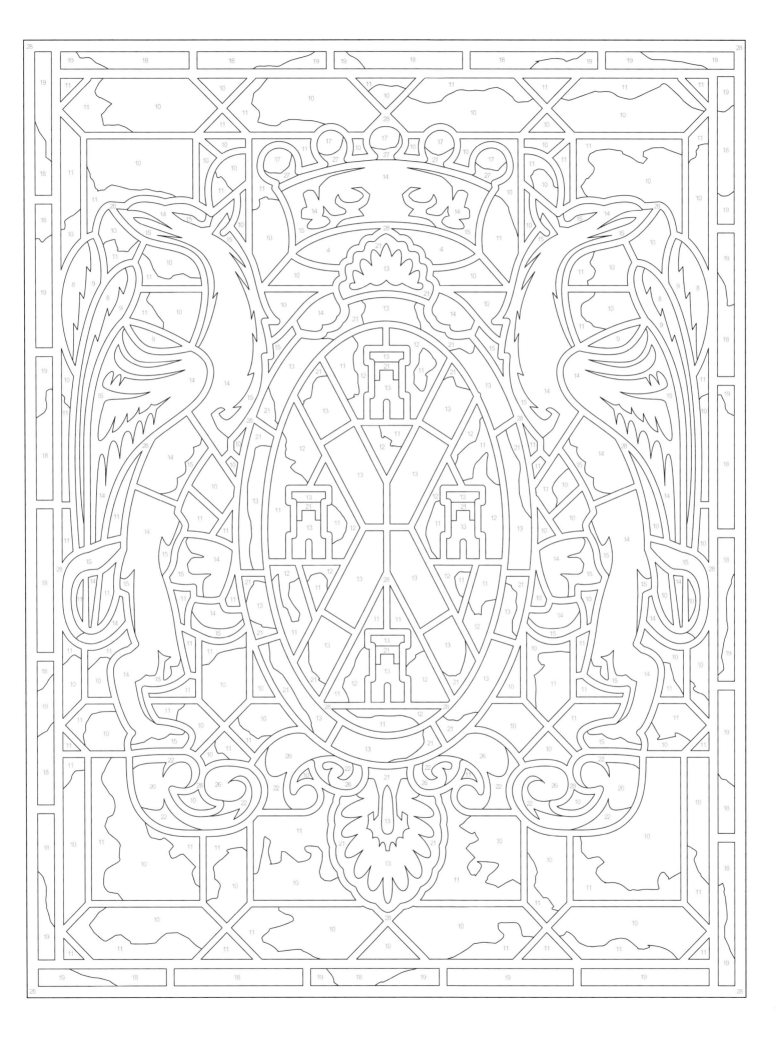

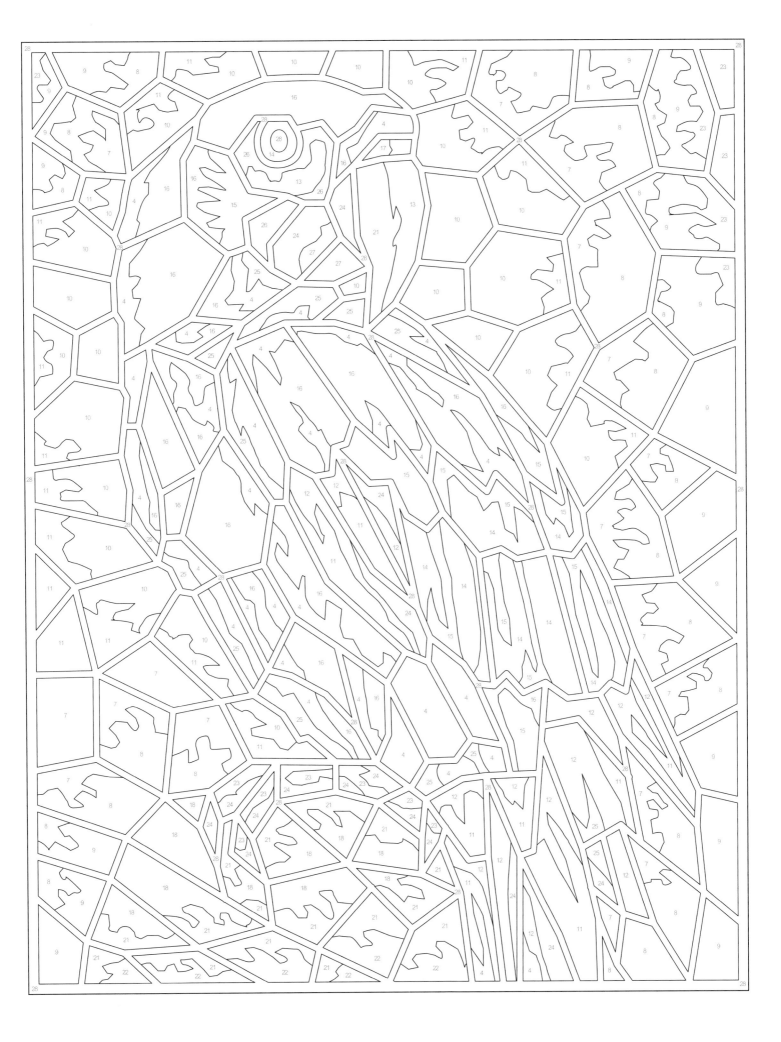

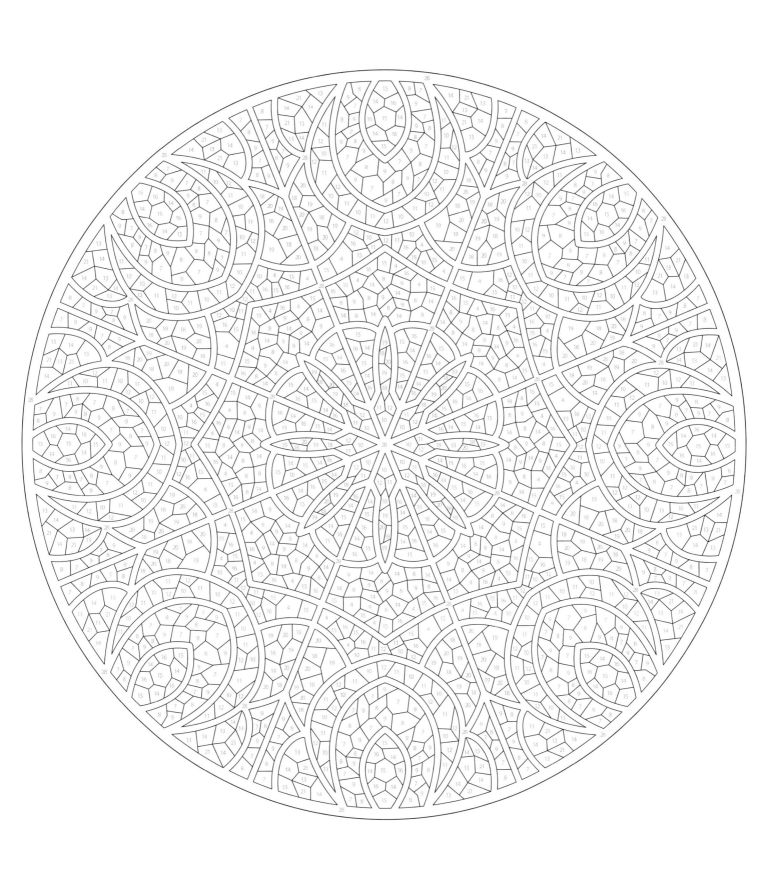

—

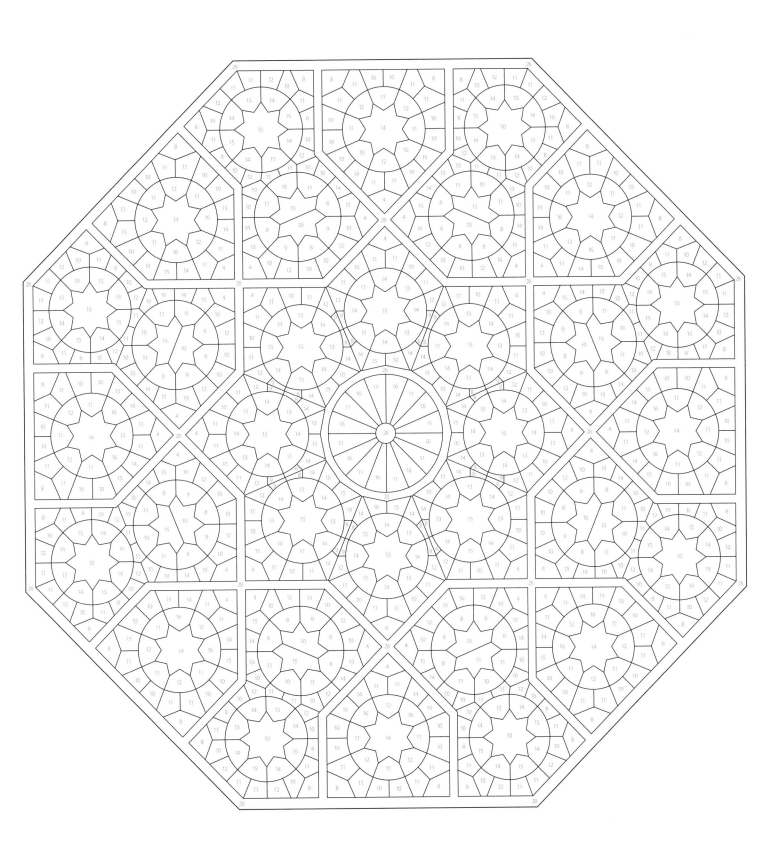